Second Edition

# PUBLIC SPEAKING HANDBOOK

## A Liberal Arts Approach

Harry C. Hazel

John S. Caputo

**KENDALL/HUNT PUBLISHING COMPANY**

4050 Westmark Drive     Dubuque, Iowa 52004-1840

# CONTENTS

# PREFACE

Most successful people have one thing in common—they can express their ideas fluently to an audience of five or five hundred. The specific purpose of this manual is to provide students in the basic course with a liberal arts approach for making better presentations. People who have prepared well can usually communicate well in a wide variety of public speaking situations.

As far back as the fourth century B.C., great scholars like Aristotle promoted wide learning as a way to effectively prepare a speech. Cicero, considered one of the greatest orators of the early Roman era, did the same. Teachers in the Renaissance envisioned an educational system that would draw upon the best learning of the past and incorporate the latest methods for students who were taking classes during the 15th century. Such students should be able to think clearly, prepare carefully and then express their ideas with force and accuracy. This approach has often been called a "liberal arts" education. Great speakers can't speak in a vacuum—they have something worthwhile to say.

The liberal arts in the 1990s provide students with a vast array of information for speeches. The study of art, history, languages, politics, philosophy, theology, science and literature gives students access to material they can share with their audiences. Electronic research devices like the internet and e-mail give public speakers today much more material to draw on for their talks.

Taking the best of the old and fusing it with new approaches and technology has some distinct advantages. These include:

◆ An overall ability to speak more eloquently in a public setting

◆ A familiarity with those research sources that help in speech preparation

◆ Better knowledge of critical thinking as it relates to public speeches

◆ A method for using stage-fright as an asset rather than a liability

◆ An appreciation for other subjects taken in a liberal arts curriculum

This handbook will give you a fuller appreciation of the liberal arts as a way of sharpening your speaking skills. You can use the book either by itself as a guide to improve public speaking or as a supplement to *Interpersonal Communication: Using Reason to Make Relationships Work*, by Caputo, Hazel and McMahon, also published by Kendall/Hunt. Often, introductory Speech courses are hybrid—they cover interpersonal, small group and public communication. Applied in the same course, the two books provide academic and practical material for all three areas.

# ACKNOWLEDGMENTS

Special thanks to Raymona Baldwin, Joann Caputo, and Kathleen Hazel for their help in preparing this handbook. We're also grateful to faculty members of the Communication Arts Department at Gonzaga University who gave us some of the material found in the appendix.

# PUBLIC SPEAKING HANDBOOK: A LIBERAL ARTS APPROACH

*Love of wisdom, then, which has helped us to discover and*
*helped us to establish all that makes Athens great,*
*which has educated us for practical affairs*
*and made gentle our relations with each other. . .*
*this love of wisdom we made manifest*
*and honored Speech*
*which all desire and envy those who know. . .*
*there is no noble and artistic speech to the wicked,*
*but it is the product of a well-knowing soul*
*and that those who use speech well are not only powerful*
*but also honored among men;*
*and to such an extent has our city outstripped the rest of*
*mankind in wisdom and speech*
*that her students have become the teachers of others. . .*
*and that those rather are called Greeks*
*who share our education than those who share our blood.*
*-Isocrates*

## INTRODUCTION

As you begin to study public speaking, it is important to understand the historical significance of speech in the development of Western culture. This historical tradition links directly with the experiences you will have in your speech class by giving a foundation for what you will learn and an added importance to your own personal development.

Rhetorical training—speech—is education for life. Since the time of the early Greeks like Plato and Aristotle, the teaching of speech has been the capstone of a liberal education.

A liberal arts education has always focused on the study of philosophy and rhetoric. Over the years, Philosophy has been divided into many sub-disciplines such as psychology, sociology, biology, etc. Rhetoric has been separated into writing (English) and speaking (Speech Communication).

As the first "democracy," Greek citizens wanted to contribute to the growth and legislative processes of their society. The ability of each citizen to speak well in public was vital. The ancient Greeks also believed that it was important to develop the ideal citizen. Greek culture, named "Paideia", undertook the character formation of the young and therefore developed a more humane culture. Rhetoric served the purpose of developing Greek culture and character — the real substance in speech training. Your participation in speech communication activities has the potential for developing culture and character; two relevant, valuable and honorable marks of a liberal education.

> *In future days, which we seek to make secure, we look forward to a world founded upon four essential freedoms. The first is freedom of speech and expression . . .*
> -*President Franklin D. Roosevelt*

# SECTION I

## *The Link Between Interpersonal Communication and Public Speaking*

> **Preview** In this section you will:
>
> ◆ Better understand why public speaking is a form of interpersonal communication.
>
> ◆ Be able to use the Canons of rhetoric for developing and giving effective speeches.-
>
> ◆ Be able to compare giving a speech with gift giving.
>
> ◆ Understand how giving a speech is a form of "polished" conversation.

Public speaking is also an interpersonal skill. The study of interpersonal communication grew rapidly after World War II, sped along by humanistic psychologists and management specialists. At the same time, scholars of rhetoric and communication developed a schism between those who studied traditional rhetoric and those who were more interested in the new social science approach to the encompassing concept of "communication." To a large extent, that schism of the 60's and 70's has begun to be erased by the notion that speech or speech communication is an interpersonal skill that connects one person to another, whether that be a single person or a mass audience. The same skills important in interpersonal communication are important in speaker audience communication. You'll recall we said that interpersonal communication involves the process of developing a relationship. Speakers must develop a relationship with their listeners.

Public speaking is one context, one setting, for interpersonal communication. Although the context for public speaking places unique demands on a speaker, these demands are not as distinct as might appear at first glance. We now turn to these demands.

# THE TRADITIONAL APPROACH: THE FIVE CANONS

The ***Rhetorica ad Herennium***, sometimes ascribed to Cicero (106-43 B.C.), provides five canons or patterns of the rhetorical system taught at Rome and Athens during the early years of Cicero. In many respects, these canons constitute the basic pattern of all theoretical and critical investigations into the art and practice of speaking. They are:

◆ ***Inventio*** (Invention) - Inventio includes the choice of a topic and the discovering of ideas and proof. At this stage of investigation, one conducts an analysis of the audience and gains a grasp of the subject matter of the speech.

◆ ***Dispositio*** (Disposition) - Dispositio includes a selection of ideas best suited for the audience, purpose and occasion for speaking, the development of a thesis and the organization of the subject matter.

◆ ***Elocutio*** (Elocution) - Elocutio includes grammatical usage, choice of language and expressive features used by a speaker. Every speech calls for a specific style of delivery and this canon helps you to select the appropriate style.

◆ ***Memoria*** (Memory) - The canon of Memoria concerns itself with the mastery of your speaking material in a sequential order. This idea explores the codes or other devices relied upon to recall your speech.

◆ ***Pronuntiatio*** (Delivery) - Pronuntiatio is the use of the voice and body in the oral presentation. Pronuntiatio includes volume, rate of speech, eye contact and gestures, appearance and dress.

These five canons provide a methodology for speech preparation and help provide the best means for delivering a speech. A former student developed an analogy of speech giving with gift giving. The gift you are giving when you give a speech is a gift of your ideas and so she extended the analogy to each of the canons.

I. **Inventio**: Finding your resources — (SHOPPING FOR THE GIFT)
    Brainstorm
    Research strategies
    Popular culture: magazines, newspapers, tv, movies.

II. **Dispositio**: Organizing your speech — (BUYING THE GIFT)
    Organization
    Theme and thesis development
    Body
    Summary
    Transitions

III. **Elocutio**:  Selecting a style — (WRAPPING THE GIFT)
>     Style
>     Tone
>     Introduction/Conclusion
>     Visual Aids

IV. **Memoria**:  Memory devices — (REMEMBERING YOUR GIFT)
>     Visual Imaging
>     Movement
>     Story
>     Note cards

V. **Pronuntiatio**: Delivery — (GIVING THE GIFT)
>     Extemporaneous
>     Vocal quality
>     Movement
>     Dress

This process of working through the five canons of rhetoric can be of great help in preparing your speech. You can see how the process moves from the idea stage to organization and delivery.  As you work through the five canons, remember that you're giving a gift; yourself.  Therefore, the process of gift giving is vital to the quality of the gift and the feelings you offer.

## CONTEMPORARY APPROACH

With the development of interpersonal communication, rhetoricians and communication scholars began to rethink the basic assumptions about public speaking. While classical rhetoric focused on the speaker, the speech and the setting, contemporary speech scholars recognized they had failed to take adequate notice of the receiver—the listener.  If you remember from Chapter One in the interpersonal book, we noted that interpersonal communication is not one-way (sender to receiver or speaker to listener) but is transactional. This means that listeners also communicate and influence the speaker.  Classical theory is speaker-oriented and contemporary theory is receiver-oriented.

Two contemporary rhetoricians who helped formulate rhetorical theories to account for this shift are I.A. Richards and Kenneth Burke. Richards believes we must have our listener understand us. For Burke, the speaker must meet the needs of the listener and speak in a way that allows the listener to identify with him or her.  This focus on the listener has created a stylistic change in public speaking.  Let's look at this change.

# Speeches As Polished Conversation

The goal in interpersonal communication is to reach a level of knowledge and sharing with another—to form a relationship. This goal is best accomplished through conversation. Although most of us are fairly comfortable in conversations with others, public speaking "seems to be different." In fact, some psychologists say the fear of public speaking is so great that many people fear public speaking more than dying from cancer. But, public speaking only "seems to be" different from conversation. In public speaking our goal should be to have a conversation with each member of our audience. In that way then, public speaking is a conversation with many people.

Although we generally don't prepare our ideas in one-to-one conversations, we do self-monitor. Sometimes we actually plan what we want to share with another person. We consider who we are talking to, what time of day would be best to speak to them, what do they already think about what we want to say, etc. We conduct an audience analysis and plan our rhetorical strategies accordingly. Think about some interpersonal conversations you planned. Remember a situation in which you asked your parents for money or to borrow the car. Or perhaps you can remember telling a loved one something he or she was not going to like to hear. Try to remember the way you analyzed your audience and how you shaped your rhetorical strategy to meet your specific goal.

This is the same task in public speaking. You ask yourself questions such as what do I know or what can I find out about my listeners that can help me communicate effectively with them? After you analyze your audience, you ask yourself how you can develop a conversation in which you can identify and come to a mutual understanding with them. In other words, you are developing a polished conversation to have with many people. To this extent then, speech is not a performance like acting, but a striving to share—to communicate with someone else. Communication requires a give-and-take transaction with another and this is best accomplished through conversation with one or many. Public speaking is both a style of and context for interpersonal communication.

# Summary

In this section we have discussed public speaking as a liberal art. We have presented both the traditional and contemporary approaches to public speaking. Lastly, we discussed the link between public speaking and interpersonal communication and described public speaking as polished conversation. In the next section, we will describe the basic challenge of public speaking and present methods for meeting that challenge.

# SECTION II

## *The Challenge of Harnessing Nervousness*

**Preview** In this section you will:

◆ Better understand what nervousness is.

◆ See how stress can work for you, rather than against you.

*"If you're nervous, don't announce it. Once you do, your audience feels obligated to worry about you. Presenters who cause worry don't inspire great confidence."*

*- Ron Hoff*

If you feel nervous about giving your first or fiftieth speech, you're in good company. Carol Burnett, Joe Montana, Barbra Streisand, and Paul Newman are four well known people who have confessed to nervousness at the prospect of speaking in public. In this section, we're going to discuss what nervousness is and how it can work *for* rather than against you.

## HARNESSING NERVOUSNESS

Fear of public speaking has received quite a few descriptions over the centuries. Some have dubbed it "stage-fright." Others more properly use the term "speech-fright." Communication instructor Isa Engleberg calls it "podium panic." Whatever the term, the feeling is familiar to almost anyone who ever gets up to face an audience. Fear can take two forms—physiological and psychological. Let's look at each.

# PHYSIOLOGICAL BASIS FOR SPEECH-FRIGHT

For most people, public speaking creates stress. Each of us is equipped with a stress mechanism that activates as soon as we perceive a threat. Most stress is brought on by a lack of **control**. If you live in a cold climate or have gone skiing, you've probably had the experience of driving along the highway and suddenly losing control of your car because you hit a patch of ice. Immediately, your stress mechanism kicked in. The pituitary gland located at the base of the brain automatically primed you for action. At the same time, your adrenal glands, located near your kidneys, started pumping blood through your body to give you the energy you needed to adapt to an emergency.

The stress mechanism can be a benefit, especially if it helps you ward off a threat. But it can also produce an unpleasant physiological reaction. Your heart beats faster and your blood surges through your veins. You might break out in a sweat. This physiological experience often disturbs public speakers the most. But if you realize that your body is reacting to a potentially stressful situation, it shouldn't be such a problem. The problem occurs when you focus on the fear and the accompanying physical symptoms rather than your audience and what you're going to say.

Hans Selye, a pioneer in the study of stress, divides the stress reaction into two categories: negative and positive. Negative stress can wear you down if you feel panicky for a long time. But the same experience can also help you. If you're excited about a particular event, like playing tennis or meeting a special someone, that physiological reaction is positive. This feeling also applies to giving a speech.

Perceptions are important here. If you see the speech as intimidating and unpleasant, stress can be negative. On the other hand, if you're prepared and have a desire to share your ideas with an audience, those perceptions can be quite positive.

# PSYCHOLOGICAL REASONS FOR STRESS

Austrian psychologist Alfred Adler proposed a theory called the inferiority complex. Adler maintains that most humans, at one time or another, believe they're inferior. This "inferiority complex" often results from the natural desire to be loved and approved. A normal amount of desire for approval is healthy. But when it becomes excessive, people who want too much approval set themselves up for failure. If you analyze **why** people feel a great fear of public speaking, it usually boils down to an apprehension about making a fool of themselves. Very few would get up to give a speech knowing the speech would be outstanding and then dread it. Most would relish the chance to do something well that makes them feel good about themselves. If they perceive a situation that could make them look foolish, they'll most likely avoid it. You might feel the same kind of fear walking into a crowded dance hall with the apprehension you might become tongue-tied when talking to other people. If you know that you're going to meet new people and have them respond to you in a positive way, that experience can be gratifying.

Many speakers fear they will lose their place in an outline or manuscript, go blank and be unable to continue. One of life's less pleasant experiences is standing alone in front of an audience and not knowing what to say next. Less fearful but still unpleasant is a speaker's belief that she or he is boring and an audience doesn't really want to hear the talk.

## THE GOOD NEWS ABOUT NERVOUSNESS: THE ENERGIZER EFFECT

As we mentioned before, even if speech-fright can be unpleasant, it can also be a great asset if used properly. One of the most comforting phenomena for speakers is the "energizer effect." The energizer effect occurs when three elements combine during a speech: the speaker is nervous, an audience is present, but the speaker has carefully prepared. Those three factors blend to make the material more vivid in the speaker's mind. Ideas become better crystallized because the pituitary gland has been activated and adrenaline is pumping through the body. Just the opposite occurs when a speaker is nervous, is facing an audience, but hasn't prepared. Then the mind tends to go blank because of the stress mechanism.

Almost always, speakers who know their material well find that the material is more vivid in their mind when they're nervous. Almost without fail, the speaker who **doesn't** know what he's talking about, finds the material fuzzy because of the same stress mechanism. Therefore, the only thing you have to fear is lack of preparation—not nervousness.

## SUMMARY

In this section, we addressed the major problem most people face in giving a speech. Nervousness is both a physiological and psychological process. It can be channeled by careful preparation through the "energizer effect." We now go on to describe the direct application of the energizer effect—the careful preparation of your talk.

# SECTION III

## *Preparing the Speech*

**Preview** In this section you will:

♦ Know how to pick a topic for your speech.

♦ See how research can be both useful and fun.

♦ Learn some ways to blend your research into your speech.

♦ Study the techniques of memory that will give you better control in front of your audience.

*"Order is Heaven's first law."*
*-Alexander Pope*

## INVENTION

"Ars est celare artem" is a famous Latin statement. It means "art is to hide art." A more modern translation might be: an expert can make a skill look easy. Graceful ballet dancers or superb athletes seem to perform without much effort. But most will tell anyone that their performance is a product of careful preparation and years of training. Giving great speeches may look easy for professionals but all will confirm that careful preparation is one of the major reasons for their success. In this section, we turn to preparation as the key to your success in delivering your talk.

## PICKING A TOPIC

This one seems easy but for many students it's one of the most difficult parts of speech preparation. Do you pick a subject you're familiar with already or do you plunge into something unfamiliar? That decision is up to you, but in general the less time you have to prepare, the more advantageous it is to pick a topic that you're somewhat familiar with already.

Make sure your approach to the topic fits what the instructor requires. For example, someone may intend at first to give a talk explaining prison reform because the assignment calls for an informative speech. Somewhere in his preparation, he gets excited about one issue he believes in and converts his report to a persuasive speech.

Once you clearly understand the assignment, you're ready to reflect on those topics that might fit the assignment. We recommend brainstorming to generate as many topics as possible. At this stage, try not to be critical of your ideas but rather generate a list of as many topics as possible.  Four criteria helpful in this process are:

a.  your interests
b.  your knowledge
c.  your audience's interests
d.  your audience's knowledge

If you have no interest in the topic, you won't deliver the speech with conviction or enthusiasm.  On the other hand, if you speak on something you're interested in but you believe your audience isn't, you must find a way to **get** them interested. Also, it is very difficult to speak about something you or your audience have little knowledge about. By keeping in mind these four considerations, you can come as close as possible to generating a topic of interest and value to yourself and your audience. Other sources of possible topics are current events that can be culled from magazines, newspapers, television, and movies. To get you started, we've listed a number of topics in the appendix.

## ANALYZING YOUR AUDIENCE

Before you get heavily into researching your topic, make sure you analyze your audience. Ask yourself about the age and knowledge level of your listeners. What might be their attitudes about the topic you're going to address? If your speech is about the advantages of using a computer instead of a typewriter or writing longhand, you would gear your material differently for a class of grade-schoolers than you would for fellow college students. If you're giving a persuasive speech, it's even more crucial to try to assess in advance the possible attitudes of your audience.

Let's say Nancy wants to give a speech advocating pro-life. A number of audience members will favor her stance on the subject. But she can also predict that a number will not. Some audience members may be neutral about the topic. For a persuasive speech, the more a speaker knows about audience attitude, the better chance she has of motivating people to accept her stance. If Mario is preparing a talk on tighter gun control to an audience of National Rifle Association members, he should pick another topic. He may experience what some researchers call the "boomerang effect." Rather than motivate people to accept his position, he hardens them in their own series of attitudes by even presenting the subject. Ideally, you would want to take a survey to assess audience's attitudes, but that's often impractical. At the very least, stop and think about how the audience would react to your subject.

Once you've thought about your audience, gather all the information you can on your topic. Although a few types of speeches can be developed from personal experience, most will require research to get a thorough knowledge of your subject.

# RESEARCH STRATEGIES

Conducting research sometimes presents us with the daunting challenge of where to begin. Research should not frighten you. In fact, research can be fun—like reading a mystery. Just as guessing "who done it" is fun in a novel, the answers you get or guess about are fun in research. Think of research as trying to get answers to your questions. Good research starts with good questions.

## *Research Through Interviews*

One of the most overlooked resources for information on a university campus are faculty. Often when students think of research, they think of the library. Every college or university has experts in almost every area of human knowledge. Taking the step to find out the areas of expertise on your campus and then setting up interviews with faculty is both informative and enjoyable. You not only gather more useful and often more current information than what is printed in books, but you meet new people and might even want to take a class with that professor someday. Also faculty can lead you to other faculty or library material you may not have been aware of. Prepare for the interview with advanced questions so you won't take too much time. Also prepare to take good notes — legible and precise — that can be used in your speech preparation and bibliography.

Another good source of information includes experts in your community. If you make an appointment to meet with a community expert, you also need to be prepared.

## *Researching in the Library*

Most college libraries have access to an almost infinite amount of information. Unfortunately, library searches can take time and there are expenses for securing material from other sources. Be sure to allow yourself enough time for adequate library searches including inter-library loans. To minimize your time involved in using the library on any basic research assignment, it helps to be familiar with how the library operates, where materials are located, how to use the computer terminals for the card catalogue and, perhaps most important, the librarians who can assist you when you need help.

When conducting research, think of an hour glass as a metaphor of your strategies. Start broadly, with general references, narrow your search with specific journal articles or books on your topic, and broaden your conclusions or generalizations you can draw from your research.

Just as note-taking is important in a personal interview, it's important when doing library research. Few things can be more frustrating than trying to find a source you used before but took inadequate notes from. We suggest the minimal information you write on a note card should contain:

1) author, title, date, and publisher. (call number as well, if you have to find it again)

2) page numbers of article

3) any quotations you copy verbatim

4) a summary of the main ideas of the material.

**Keep** all your note cards from both interviews and library research. You'll need them when you construct a bibliography of the resources you consulted. Be accurate and give proper credit to your sources. Improperly citing sources of information can lead to **plagiarism**. Plagiarism is the unlawful act of stealing or attempting to pass off another's work as your own. It denies the exclusive rights of the owner and materially impairs these rights and the value of the work. When you use someone else's ideas, but don't say whose ideas they are, that is plagiarism. If you plagiarize, even accidentally, it can have serious consequences. These consequences can range from a stern warning, failure on an assignment, or in extremely serious cases, dismissal from the University, or being brought to court. Remember intellectual honesty is important and your professors view solid research very favorably, so don't spoil it with misidentification of sources.

## The Bibliography

Most of your professors will require you to submit a bibliography or list of references with your speech. Most often this will be part of your outline. Speech teachers generally require one of two formats for bibliographies. This format may be the same or different from what you are learning in your English composition class. The two most used formats are the APA Style (American Psychological Association) and the MLA (Modern Language Association). Be sure to check with your professor about what style she or he wants. The main goal is to be consistent and accurate. See Appendix H for details of correct bibliographic formatting.

# BLENDING RESEARCH INTO YOUR SPEECH

Let's turn now to a practical application of applying research to your subject. We present an outline of an informative speech. We then go through the steps of research and organization used to prepare the report. The speech is an explanation of how John F. Kennedy's careful preparation before the first presidential debate in September of 1960 helped him win the presidency. The talk also deals with Richard Nixon's lack of preparation as a factor in his defeat. The works cited are in MLA format.

The speaker initially thought about discussing the entire Kennedy-Nixon campaign but the assignment called for a 6 to 8 minute speech. Therefore, he narrowed his topic to a single event which unfolded over two days and researched that in depth. In preparing the speech, he took the following steps:

1. He wrote a one page outline based on what he already knew about the topic.

2. About a fourth of the way down the page, he wrote a thesis sentence—i.e., preparation was the key factor in the first debate between Kennedy and Nixon.

3. He then broke down the thesis sentence to two major Roman numerals:

I. Preparation by Kennedy

II. Preparation by Nixon.

4. Then he went back and, under Roman I, decided to cover what Kennedy did on Sunday and Monday. So he wrote those down as capital letters in an outline. He did the same for his second Roman numeral.

5. As he did his research, he read some sources about the debate. He also looked up newspaper articles and kept fleshing out the short outline.

6. When he finished the body of the outline, he thought about a specific lead for the introduction. He knew that an introduction should get the attention of the audience and should help establish rapport. In considering his own speaking experiences, he remembered a recurring nightmare. The dream involved himself getting a part in a play and then going before an audience on opening night without knowing his lines. This introduction would serve two purposes: it would be a better attention-getter than an announcement of the topic, and it would personalize the speech by helping to establish a rapport with his audience.

7. He then wrote his conclusion. In the conclusion, he used the "echo effect"—a reference to the nightmare he mentioned in the introduction.

Purpose: To report on a significant event that underscores the need for careful speech preparation.

## INTRODUCTION

I.  Every once in a while, I have a nightmare I would prefer to skip:

    A.  I've been given a part in a play, but I haven't really learned my lines.

    B.  It is opening night and I'm expected to perform.

    C.  One of the worst experiences for public speakers is having to deliver a speech without proper preparation.

II.  Our most controversial President learned this painful lesson in September of 1960—the evening of the first presidential debate between Richard Nixon and John Kennedy.

## BODY

Thesis Sentence: The deciding factor in the first Kennedy-Nixon debate was the preparation by both candidates.

I.  Preparation of Kennedy: (White 311)

    A.  Sunday, September 25

        1.  JFK arrived at the Ambassador East Hotel with his three "brain trust" advisors, Sorenson, Goodwin and Feldman.
            a.  Ted Sorenson was a speech writer and chief tactician.
            b.  Richard Goodwin was a brilliant young lawyer.
            c.  Mike Feldman was a law instructor and later a successful business man.

        2.  The four brought with them a portable library of information on any topic that might come up during the debate.
            a.  They put in a long session, preparing for the debate like college students getting ready for an exam.
            b.  Each stressed the latest information.

    B.  Monday, September 26

        1.  The four spent another skull session in the morning.

        2.  JFK then had lunch with Sorenson, Robert Kennedy and the public opinion analyst Louis Harris.

        3.  After lunch, Kennedy gave a brief speech to the United Brotherhood of Carpenters.

        4.  He took a nap until five when he woke up refreshed.

        5.  Put in another study session.

        6.  He then ate what he termed a "splendid dinner" by himself in his room.

    C.  Preparation at the Chicago TV studio:

        1.  JFK inspected the set.

        2.  He had worn a dark suit to contrast with the gray studio background.

        3.  Sent back for a light blue shirt since studio advisors indicated that a white shirt would glare under the lights.

        4.  Had no make-up

II.  Nixon's preparation

    A.  Sunday:

        1.  Although Nixon had been advised to arrive in Chicago a day early to rest, he disregarded the advice and arrived tired at the Pic-Congress Hotel late Sunday night.

        2.  Aides had tried to reach Herb Klein, Nixon's chief advisor, but Klein could not be found.

    B.  Monday

        1.  Nixon gave a speech to the United Brotherhood of Carpenters during the morning—a speech which Nixon felt was not favorably received.

        2.  The rest of the day Nixon spent by himself, mostly in his hotel room.
           a.  TV advisors could not get in to see him.
           b.  He received one visitor for five minutes.
           c.  Henry Cabot Lodge called long distance to try to destroy the "assassin image."

        3.  Preparation at the Studio:
           a.  Nixon struck his already injured knee when he got out of the car and his face turned pale white.
           b.  Nixon inspected the set.
           c.  One advisor applied a light pancake make-up called "Lazy-Shave" to hide Nixon's five o'clock shadow.

## CONCLUSION

I.  The results of that first crucial debate are history, but most experts agree that Kennedy won. (Freely 398).

    A.  The Committee on the 1960 Presidential Campaign—an impartial group—stated that JFK won by a vote of 20 to 6.

    B.  All but one of the Committee agreed that Kennedy had made the greatest political gain.

    C.  *The New York Times* stated that the debates were "really the deciding factors" in Kennedy's victory. (1)

II.   The performance of each candidate underscores the importance of speech preparation.

A.   A carefully prepared talk can be richly satisfying.

B.   One that is not can be a living nightmare.

### Works Cited

Freely, Austin. *Argumentation and Debate.* New York: Wadsworth, 1966.

"Now the Vote: The Campaign." *The New York Times* November 6, 1960:1.

White, Theodore. *The Making of the President.* New York: Atheneum, 1961.

In constructing your outline, remember to start with your **thesis sentence.** This becomes the anchor for your speech and should include a summary of your main points—as you saw in the preceding outline. Everything else flowed from the thesis that preparation was crucial in the outcome of the first Kennedy-Nixon debate.

Write your **introduction** after you've fleshed out the major points from your central idea sentence. Since the purpose of the introduction is to get the attention of your audience and help you establish rapport with them, you need to know how your topic is developed before you can come up with a "grabber." Typical introductions include stories, challenges or quotations. Brief stories that relate directly to your topic work well because they follow a chronological order and are easy to remember. Almost everyone will listen to a good story. For example, if you're demonstrating how to shoot free throws, you could tell your audience about the time you were in a tie game with two seconds left and you went to the line to sink—or miss—the winning shots.

A **conclusion** serves two purposes. It summarizes the key points of the talk and ties it together, preferably with a compelling final sentence. If you memorize just one line of your speech, make it the conclusion. Some speakers hover like a plane trying to find a landing strip before they conclude their speech. Conclusions should be specific and should leave the audience with a memorable thought about the theme. For example, let's say a speaker is giving a talk on the importance of self-image and how one's thoughts shape the feeling of confidence. After developing the speech, she could use a quotation attributed to Henry Ford: "Whether you believe you **can** or believe you **can't**, you're right." That sentence has the double advantage of cementing the thoughts of the speech and providing a specific ending.

Some speakers conclude by saying "thank you" to the audience. Most experts suggest that a speaker simply pause before the final sentence, recite the final point, smile and then stand there and answer questions—if questions are appropriate. If the occasion does not call for questions, walk back to your desk. The principle behind not thanking the audience is that you're doing them a favor by sharing your information. This is not a hard and fast rule because some speakers feel more comfortable saying something like "thanks for allowing me to share these ideas with you." Anything specific that will bring the speech to a conclusion and create a warm rapport with the audience is acceptable.

The outline of the Kennedy-Nixon debate is designed for a relatively short speech. If the speaker had tried to talk about the entire campaign in 1960, he would be covering too much material. Many students get an assignment to deliver a three to five minute speech and prepare enough to go for twenty minutes. Let's say Brad has chosen "skiing" as a topic. As he prepares, he plans to talk about ski equipment, snow-plow and parallel turns, stopping, and what to look for in a fun lodge after a day on the slopes. He's trying to cram too much into the timeframe he has. While it may be helpful to have **slightly** more material than you can use, don't over-do it.

***Trust your well prepared outline rather than a memorized manuscript.***

Student speakers who write an outline **plus** a manuscript and then speak from a manuscript are creating extra work for themselves. If you use vivid imaging to remember the key points of your outline, you won't have to use a manuscript. Words by themselves tend to be abstract and hard to remember. As we mentioned before, clearly grafted images in your mind are far easier to recall, especially if they're in outline form. If you vividly imagine beforehand the speech setting and use effective memory techniques, you'll be just fine when you deliver your talk.

Some teachers suggest taking the key ideas from your outline and putting them on note cards. The point is: know the material well, but don't try to memorize every word. Almost always, you'll be in greater control and will reduce stress if you use guided vivid imagery to remember the key points of your speech. Let's turn to a more detailed discussion of memory and the vivid imagery method.

# MEMORIA

Treatises on memory have been around for a long time. In his book **De Oratore**, the first century Roman politician and well known speaker Cicero discusses various ways to remember speeches. Over the centuries, many other experts have offered helpful tips for speakers who want to have control over their material. Let's look at some of these techniques.

## How the Memory Works: Vivid Imaging

The mind is an amazing mechanism. Not only can we think, but the central nervous system also allows us to remember events from the past. Faculty psychologists of the 19th century used to divide the human mind into compartments—one for cognition, another for memory, another for sensing, another for sight, etc. More recent research has shown that the human mind is much more complicated than that and often cognition blends into imagination. But for the purpose of explaining the vivid imaging system, we can make a distinction between cognition and imagination. When you think about an abstract concept, you don't necessarily have to have an image in your mind. For example, when a teacher says "loyalty is a virtue", you know what she's talking about. Below are some other examples of cognitive type statements:

◆ five plus seven equals twelve

◆ honesty is the best policy

◆ Jean Paul Sartre was an existentialist

◆ women often make better leaders than men

◆ reading is a more complicated process than watching television

You can understand those abstract thoughts, but you'll remember them much better if you form a vivid image of each one.

Think of a movie you've seen recently—or even a year ago. If someone asked you to describe the plot and the characters, you could probably do so easily. You form pictures in your mind. This is what we mean by "vivid imaging." Vivid imaging is a process of clearly seeing in your imagination a scene before it occurs. Imagination is different from intellect. Our intellects allow us to think of abstract ideas like the ones just listed. Our mind can make the connection between the two ideas, but it's hard to form a picture. For example, I could say: "the car was in an accident." A statement like that is less difficult to understand than the one about Jean Paul Sartre. But it's still abstract. If I asked you to **imagine** a 1987 Oldsmobile Cutlass slamming into a telephone pole, you would probably remember it better. If I **showed** you a picture or a video of a Cutlass crashing into the pole and then asked you to remember it five minutes later, you would recall it even more vividly. The point is: the more you use your imagination along with your thoughts, the clearer the material will be to you. Let's apply that to giving a speech.

If we asked you to think of yourself before you deliver your talk as calm and prepared, you could do that. But if we suggested you to vividly imagine yourself walking from your chair in the classroom to the lectern or podium, pausing, and then starting with a very specific introduction, you would have a better chance of remembering. Abstract ideas are like Teflon—they often don't stick. If you use the velcro of vivid imagination, you can remember concepts much better. We suggest two ways you can use vivid imaging to help you deliver an effective speech. The first relates to advance preparation and the second can be applied to remembering the key ideas in your talk.

## LONG-RANGE PREPARATION

As soon as you're assigned a specific date to give a talk, imagine yourself as somewhat nervous but in total command because you've prepared so thoroughly. Vividly imagine yourself walking to the front of the room addressing the audience, establishing eye contact and talking with expertise on your subject. Some people find it helpful to **meditate** in the few days before they give a speech. Meditation helps them focus and reduce stress.

The following tip may appear negative at first, but many professional speakers find it helpful. Imagine in advance the **worst** that could happen when you deliver a talk. Most people think the worst experience would be going blank and not knowing what to say next. Play out in your mind what you would do if you go blank. See yourself pausing for a few seconds, looking at your outline and finding out where you were, and then continuing to speak. In the unlikely event that the worst happens, you have a plan.

## DIRECT PREPARATION

You're now ready to apply vivid imaging to direct preparation. Remember that the more you use your imagination, the better chance you have of mastering the material for your talk. If you've been impressed with people who have a superb memory, they probably use three basic methods—**association, imagination** and **repetition**. Association is a linking of vivid images in your mind and repeating them enough times so you remember them well. An example of this process might help. Suppose someone asked you to try to repeat the following unrelated items: the movie character ET, a blue sport coat, a yellow Volkswagen, a pine tree, a telephone pole, a brick, a cup of coffee, blue suede shoes, broken glass, an angry librarian, an elevator and a glass door. Could you easily repeat those terms? Probably not. Now try this. Picture in your mind as graphically as you can the movie character from Steven Speilberg's movie. Now see ET driving a yellow Volkswagen in front of a library. He parks his yellow Volkswagen between a pine tree and a telephone pole. On the passenger seat is a brick. ET picks up the brick gets out of his Volkswagen, goes up the steps of the library, comes to the glass door and hurls the brick through the glass door. A librarian is sitting behind the glass door wearing blue suede shoes. Behind this person is an elevator. The brick crashes through the glass door striking the coffee the librarian is drinking and spills all over his blue suede shoes. In anger, the librarian picks up the brick and throws it back at ET who scrambles down the steps littered with broken glass and leaps into his yellow Volkswagen still parked between a pine tree and a telephone pole. He then drives off. If you repeated that series of images two or three times, notice how much easier it would be to talk about it. You will have applied the principles of memory. You linked some vivid images. You then repeated them so that you saw the images firmly entrenched in the memory section of your mind.

Apply the same technique as you prepare to remember your speech. Recall the speech on the Kennedy-Nixon debate preparation. If a speaker vividly saw herself on stage on opening night without knowing her lines, she could easily tell that to an audience. Then she would go to her central idea sentence and get a clear idea of Kennedy and Nixon preparing. Then she would link that image to the next image about Kennedy. The speaker would have a picture in her mind of the candidate checking into the Ambassador East Hotel. She might even see a neon sign over the hotel flashing "Ambassador East." If she can see the three people who accompanied Kennedy, Ted Sorenson, Richard Goodwin, and Mike Feldman, all the better. She would link that image to the four of them studying for the debate, using information from a portable chest they brought for the occasion. She would then link that image to the Monday morning study session with the assistants firing questions at Kennedy and Kennedy responding. That image would be linked to Kennedy having lunch and giving a speech to the United Brotherhood of Carpenters. For your own speech, get some vivid images, see them locked together as a series of incidents like the "ET example" and you have a much better chance of remembering.

One other technique that reinforces this method is to take a yellow highlighter and mark in those words that are the most vivid in your imagination. If you're speaking and you momentarily forget where you are, glance at the outline and the highlighted words will stand out from the others on the page. Let's say our speaker has finished talking about what Kennedy did on Sunday, but she can't quite remember what he did on Monday. She looks at her outline, and sees the word "study session" underlined. That word flashes the image she needs to continue.

## REHEARSAL

Speakers have a variety of ways to rehearse their speech. A few people like to practise in front of a mirror—although many find this approach artificial. Others deliver the speech to a roommate or friend. Still others tape record the speech and play it back a number of times until they're satisfied they have a solid grasp of the material. Some play out in their mind the scene of the talk and then mentally connect the various images they're going to discuss. Use whatever approach you find works for you, but make sure you practice your speech at least 3 to 5 times.

## SUMMARY

In this section, we've looked at some ways to prepare your talk, both long-range and short term. Because thorough preparation is the key to effective speaking, we've stressed the importance of analyzing your audience. We went on to show you how to conduct research both in and out of the library. We then discussed ways to apply your research to the construction of your outline. Finally, we discussed some tested methods of memory. We now move on to aspects of delivery that will make your speech as effective as possible.

# SECTION IV

## *Delivering the Speech*

**Preview** In this section you will:

◆ Examine how the various components of delivery can make you a better speaker.

◆ Look at the various nonverbal elements that can affect your presentation.

◆ Learn how visual aids can enhance your talk.

*"The manner of your speaking is full as important as the matter, as more people have ears to be tickled than understandings to judge."*

*Philip Chesterfield*

## DELIVERING THE SPEECH (PRONUNCIATIO)

Some speakers can talk about the most intriguing subjects but are dull because they speak in a monotone. Others can speak on the hazards of lint in a clothes dryer and make their subject come alive. Outstanding speakers usually are adept at delivery, as well as organization and content. Let's look now at some elements of delivering your speech effectively to an audience. You'll want to be aware of at least five vocal elements: projection, rate, vocal quality, inflection, and articulation.

## PROJECTION

Projection is a combination of volume and vocal energy. The two are different. Some speakers can be loud but can still sound dull. Other speakers can talk softly but have such energy in their voice that they compel our attention. The combination of the two is usually best. General Douglas MacArthur gave a speech many years ago that rings in the minds of those who heard it. President Harry Truman had lifted MacArthur's command in Korea and the General returned to the United States and gave two speeches—one in New York and another at West Point. Anyone who has heard either one of those speeches on a recording is struck by the way MacArthur delivered his talk. The General was dramatic, energetic and extremely effective with both audiences. Certainly his ideas were important, but his delivery made the ideas seem especially memorable.

As you think about delivering your own speech in class, increase projection more than you think you should. Many speakers do just the opposite. Because they're nervous, they tend to speak **softer** than usual. Projection during a speech has at least two advantages. You sound more dynamic to the audience and you rechannel physical nervousness.

Think for a moment about the process of projection. To speak, you take a gulp of air and store it momentarily in your lungs. As you start to speak, the air leaves your lungs, travels up the trachea, strikes the vocal bands located in the larynx (the top of your larynx is your Adam's apple or thorax). From there the sound spreads through the three chambers of your throat, mouth and nasal passage. If you're speaking softly, you'll probably experience, as most speakers do, the normal symptoms of nervousness—faster heart beat and muscle tension. Stronger projection will help dissipate those symptoms. If you speak softly, you can literally **feel** the nervousness more acutely than if you speak with force.

One of the authors took a speech class a number of years ago from a teacher named Art Quine. Art promoted the advantages of a strong projection. As an exercise, he had students give what he called a "fanatic speaker talk." Each student had to bring a rolled-up piece of newspaper and face the audience as he or she delivered a talk. Art, the instructor, would stand behind the speaker. He had instructed the audience members before-hand to boo and hiss when he raised his hands. A typical topic might be "Broccoli is one of the healthiest and most delicious foods you can eat." The speaker's job was to project his voice over the din of the audience as they booed and hissed. After about thirty-five seconds, Art would lower his hands as a signal to be quiet. The speaker was supposed to keep projecting his voice. Art would then stop and ask the speaker how he felt physiologically when he kept projecting his voice. Could he **feel** the nervousness as much as he did when he spoke softly? Most speakers would reply no. Even though they were speaking in fun to a "hostile audience", their nervousness had dissipated as a result of the greater projection.

Project your voice more than you think you have to. You'll sound better to the audience and you'll also feel less nervous. Projection does not mean that you shout or vocally badger the audience, but it does mean you inject enthusiasm into your delivery.

# RATE

If speaking with more projection is important, so is a slower rate. Because of the adrenaline pouring through their bodies, most speakers tend to speak more rapidly than they should. If you slow down, you can take advantage of the differential between thought speed and voice speed. While you typically speak at around 125 words per minute during conversation, your mind races at 400 to 500 words per minute. This allows you to listen to what the other person is saying, reflect on it, prepare a response and keep the conversation going. The faster you speak, the harder it is to think ahead. If you start your speech at the rate 150 words per minute, it's hard to slow down. Tell yourself to speak at around 100 words per minute. Then you'll have more time to think about what you're going to say next and to focus on faces in the audience. Occasionally, student speakers will talk too slowly but the slow speaker is the exception.

To apply this point about slower rate, think of professional speakers like Diane Sawyer, Jane Pauley, Mike Wallace, or Peter Jennings. When you listen carefully, you'll notice that their rate is calm, measured, and relaxed. Many who speak rapidly sound tense. As you mentally prepare for your talk, tell yourself that you're going to go slower than usual. When you practice with a friend or on a tape recorder or in front of a mirror, go slower. The natural adrenaline during the speech will propel you to speak faster so any kind of slowing down process will probably help you. Some student speakers find it helpful to write SLOW DOWN in capital letters at the top of each page of their outline.

# VOCAL QUALITY

If projection helps tame speech-fright and rate gives you more control, **quality** helps make your presentation sound more pleasant. Most of us don't really know how we sound when we talk—even though everyone else does. Sound waves bounce off walls or run through our cranium. Neither give us an accurate perception of how our voice sounds to others. If our voice is a primary index of our personality, the sound of the voice can either add to or detract from the effect we have on an audience. Some people have voices that are warm and pleasant. Others sound harsh and abrasive. We're usually more aware of someone who has a grating, abrasive voice. An unpleasant voice may not have the same effect as screeching fingernails across the blackboard, but it can impact the overall effect of your speech.

The quality of your voice is a combination of several factors. After a rush of air strikes your vocal bands, it disperses through your throat, mouth, and nasal passage. If those three chambers are constricted, you'll tend to have a higher sound than if you take full advantage of these natural amplifiers. Try this test. Record your voice in a conversation or during a practice speech. Do you like what you hear? If you don't, there are ways to change the sound of your voice. Experiment by letting the sound roll around your nasal passage and mouth. Keep working at it until you're satisfied with the quality of your sound. Be careful of getting discouraged. Most people don't like the sound of their voice when they first hear it. But, with constant homework during conversation and practice on a tape recorder, they realize that quality can be improved.

## INFLECTION

Effective speakers like Paula Zahn and Jesse Jackson sound enthusiastic about whatever topic they're discussing. Part of this stems from their vocal projection but they also use inflection well. Inflection is the vocal variety a speaker uses. Most good speakers use plenty of variety as they discuss a topic or give a speech. Varied inflection is the opposite of a monotone. Some speakers have very little vocal variety. They can have the best ideas in the world, but if they transmit little vocal variety, an audience can quickly get bored.

## ARTICULATION

Articulation refers to how distinctly a speaker enunciates words. Articulation is not the same as **pronunciation**. If I mispronounce a word, I may put the accent on the wrong syllable or I may mangle the accepted usage. If a speaker said "I just had a very **un**ique experience", with emphasis on the first syllable, he's mispronouncing. Lack of articulation often includes slurring syllables which makes it difficult for audiences to understand what a speaker is saying. Some professional speakers like Paul Harvey can get away with speaking very rapidly because their articulation is so distinct.

Articulation is not an easy skill to develop and practice. In a conversation, many of us speak with slurred diction. It's harder to do that during a public talk. One of the best ways to improve articulation is to practice exercises that make you move your lips, mouth, and tongue with more vigor than usual. Professor Henry Higgins in the musical "My Fair Lady" worked with Eliza Doolittle to improve her pronunciation and her articulation. He made her say "The rain in Spain lays mainly on the plain" over and over until her words were understandable to the normal Brit. Many professional speakers exaggerate pronunciation during a practice session. Once they get before an audience, the practice helps them sound more distinct.

## PUTTING TOGETHER ALL THE VOCAL ELEMENTS

Most effective speakers are able to blend all five elements into a seamless vocal tapestry. They're energetic enough to sound interesting, they speak slowly enough to be easily heard, and their variety is such that it's a pleasure to listen to what they're saying. Their voice quality is pleasant and they enunciate words clearly enough so that listeners don't miss a syllable.

Most professional speakers make it sound easy when they deliver their talks. But what looks easy has taken years to develop and hone. Such speakers reflect the story of the traveler who arrived in New York City looking for Carnegie Hall. After a half hour, he noticed an elderly, stooped man with a violin case coming out of a doorway. He went up to the man and said "Sir, can you tell me how to get to Carnegie Hall?" The little old man straightened up, raised his right fist and said "**Practice, practice, practice!**" The more you practice, the better your voice will sound to an audience. And you can practice every day during conversation. The rewards are well worth the effort.

## Nonverbal Elements of a Speech

### Dress

You've done your homework. Now it's time to consider your appearance as you get ready for your speech. What should you wear? Each instructor will have specific guidelines for what to wear, but here are some suggestions.

Remember that the way you look has a direct impact on your audience, especially when you start to speak. Anything that distracts can affect your performance. Baseball hats turned backward, shirt hanging out from pants, loud clothes or ripped jeans can create a negative effect. In general, dress at least a notch above members of the audience. If most are wearing casual clothes, make sure that yours are neat and of good quality. You may not want to give your talk in a formal dress or a three piece suit, but at least look sharp. For some speeches—like a persuasive talk—the more formal outfit of dress for women and sport-coat/tie for men is appropriate and will add to your overall positive image.

### Posture

Stand straight, tall and confident—even if you don't feel that way at first. Avoid slumping over the lectern. Be careful of pacing back and forth. While some speakers feel more comfortable sitting on the front part of a desk to project a more casual look, most of the time you're better off standing straight.

### Gestures

One of the more colorful eras in public speaking was the Elocutionary period in the late 1800s. During this time, teachers of speech emphasized the exaggerated use of gestures for public speakers. Students had to describe exactly what gesture they were going to use on what syllable of a particular word. We won't do that in this handbook. But we want to provide some simple guidelines for using gestures.

Speakers can distract an audience either because they use awkward, exaggerated gestures or virtually no gestures at all. In the first instance, a speaker might be waving wildly or pointing an index finger at the wrong time. At the other extreme, a speaker might stand stiffly in front of the audience with both hands clutched in front, in back or in both pockets. As a basic rule, any nonverbal cue that distracts should be avoided. Any gesture that reinforces what you're saying is appropriate. If you find it helpful, hold onto the lectern as you start your talk. If a gesture seems appropriate, let it happen.

## Audio/Visual Aids

You've now prepared your speech by putting it in outline form. What about using audio/visual aids? The answer to that question of course depends on the kind of speech you're giving and what visual aids might help make your talk more clear or persuasive. You can strengthen almost any kind of speech with audio/visual aids. Let's discuss some of their advantages.

Blending your speech with visual aids tends to make the material stick longer in the eyes or minds of the audience. Let's say you're giving a presentation about Napoleon's defeat at Waterloo in 1815. Certainly you can simply talk about what happened to the beleaguered French commander. But if you tell and **show** your audience, they'll more likely remember what you say. If you talk about Napoleon and also show a picture of him plus a map where the battle was fought, your audience will better remember what you said.

## Types of Visual Aids

You have a variety of visual audio aids for almost any speech you want to give. If you're demonstrating how to swing a golf club, you would be well advised to bring in two or three clubs along with a plastic ball and a tee. (Real golf balls tend to break windows during speeches.) If you're demonstrating easy steps in playing the guitar, bring along the guitar and play a tune to illustrate your basic points.

If you were giving a persuasive speech about the hazards of chewing tobacco, you could use "Mr. Dip Lip"—a rubberized model of the human head, larynx and chest to graphically illustrate what happens when someone chews snuff.

One of the more common visual aids is a viewgraph displayed on an overhead. You need to prepare such viewgraphs in advance and make sure the letters or figures are large enough for the audience to see easily. Sometimes slides help highlight your topic. Let's say you're going to give a persuasive speech on why students ought to consider studying abroad during their junior year. Slides of Florence, Italy and an opening tour through Germany and Austria can make a presentation sparkle.

If you're trying to explain to the class how a military trial takes place, you could begin with a one minute cutting of the trial scene from "A Few Good Men." Rented videos are readily available and short clips can make your talk more graphic.

Maps or posters are other items you could use to illustrate your subject. If you were giving a talk on the advantages of regular aerobic exercise, you might bring in posters of vibrant looking people involved in brisk exercise.

Even self-drawn aids on the black board can be a help in making the material stick in the minds of your audience. Don't worry about your artistic skill, as long as the drawing is clear.

If you're going to use any kind of audiovisual aid, here are some tips to make sure they support rather than inhibit your talk.

1. **Prepare beforehand.**

   Few things are more frustrating for a speaker than a visual aid that fails to work. Let's say you've prepared a viewgraph explaining the advantages of driving an economy car. You have had the viewgraph professionally done, but have never tested the overhead projector before giving your talk. You'll have far more peace of mind by testing the machine before class to make sure the light works and the picture is lined up properly on the screen. It also helps to anticipate in advance that the machine won't work and to have a contingency plan if that happens.

2. **Keep your aids simple.**

   The primary purpose of a visual/audio aid is to illustrate in more graphic detail what you're saying in the speech. If you're talking about the advantages of investing in the stock market and you bring in a complicated, difficult-to-read chart about how stocks work, you could defeat your purpose.

3. **Have the aid visible only when you're making a specific point about the object you're demonstrating.**

   If you're giving a talk about the glories of visiting England and Ireland in the spring, make sure the viewgraph or slide matches the point you're talking about at the time. For example, if you finish talking about England in the spring and have a slide of London showing all through your explanation of Dublin's charm, you'll distract your audience. Or if you have a picture of Arnold Palmer teeing off with a wood during a discussion of putting, your talk will seem disjointed.

4. **Talk to your audience and not the aid.**

It's easy to talk directly to the visual aid while you're showing it rather than to your audience. If a speaker has written something on the board and then has his back to the audience while he's speaking, it's harder to hear him. If you can't turn and directly face the audience, at least stand sideways so you can make reference both to the aid and to your listeners.

## SUMMARY

In this section, we've discussed the elements of "elocutio" or the delivery of a speech. We emphasized that your voice can be a powerful instrument in getting your message across to an audience. Such an impact can be strengthened by how you dress, stand and use gestures. Audio/visual aids can be a great help, especially in informative speeches. We provided some guidelines for proper use of these aids. We now go on to describe the various kinds of speeches you'll be required to deliver in class.

# SECTION V

## Different Kinds of Speeches

**Preview** In this section, you will:

- ◆ Discover the various approaches to public speaking.

- ◆ Understand the differences and similarities between informative, demonstrative and persuasive speeches.

- ◆ Learn more about speeches for special occasions.

- ◆ Study some different types of group presentations.

*"Oratory is an art, not a science, and a great rhetorician may choose to grab, slug, provoke or tickle."*

*William Safire*

In your speech class, the instructor will most likely ask you to give several **extemporaneous** speeches. These are talks that require thorough preparation and organization, but are not memorized. A second type is the **manuscript** speech. Here the speaker writes a talk word for word and delivers it usually from memory. At the opposite end of the spectrum is the **impromptu** speech. Here the speaker is given a topic and must speak on it immediately or within a minute or two. Let's talk about the pros and cons of each kind of speech.

## EXTEMPORANEOUS

In this assignment, your instructor lets you pick a topic and you prepare for it in advance. When you deliver the speech, you use an outline as a reference if you can't maintain eye contact with your audience the whole time. (Most experienced speakers at least **glance** at their outline occasionally.) Unless you're giving a talk for some very formal occasion where you want absolute precision of language, the well organized outline is your best support system. If you lose your place for a second or two, you can always look down and catch one of the highlighted words you've marked as part of the vivid imaging method we discussed before.

## MEMORIZED MANUSCRIPT

As we just mentioned, the memorized manuscript may be suitable for occasions that demand precise language. Or if you have the luxury of access to a teleprompter, you may want to speak from the text reflected at eye level. But for most speeches, the manuscript method is difficult. If you lose your place with just one word, it's hard to quickly get back on track. The memorized speech can also sound wooden and un-natural if you're not used to delivering it.

## IMPROMPTU

Probably the most challenging speech for anyone is the impromptu speech. A rela-tive at a family gathering asks you to say "a few words about our family." You have less than a minute to collect your thoughts. You may be asked to give an impromptu speech in class. If you do, we have some suggestions about how to deliver it with skill.

In the minute—or even few seconds—you have to prepare, think of a single thought you can build stories around. For example, if you really were asked to talk about "our family," on your way to the spot you're going to speak, think of something like: our family is always there when we need them in a crisis (assuming that's true). Then think of a story about one family member who illustrates that theme. Stories are easy to remember and tell. Abstract ideas can be fuzzy and hard to talk about. When you've quickly assembled the theme and a story or two, think of a **simple** introduc-tion. For example, you could tell your audience of relatives that you're really glad to see them again. Then conclude simply. You could say "thanks for allowing me the opportunity to share a few thoughts with you." If the muse of inspiration gives you more to say, fine. But don't worry about being eloquent.

Another tactic experienced impromptu speakers use is to draw upon a selection of stories they've saved and put in a file. Stories make a speech come alive and can be applied in a number of situations. Let's illustrate that point with a story, instead of leaving you with the abstract principle that collected stories are useful.

Jewish story-teller Steve Sanfield, in his cassette tape *"Can This Be Paradise?,"* tells about Jacob Ben Wolfe Kranz who was regarded as a great orator and teacher. One of his friends asked Jacob how he managed to find the right parable for virtually any situation. Rather than respond with a lengthy explanation, Jacob told the follow-ing story.

Once there was a Russian nobleman who wanted to be the greatest archer alive. Although he had worked hard to develop his reputation as one of the finest archers in the empire, he still wanted to perfect the art. One day as he was traveling past a small Jewish town, he noticed an old barn. On the wall were a dozen crudely painted targets. And in the middle of each bullseye was an arrow. The nobleman was astounded. Never before had he seen such accuracy. So he had the one responsible brought before him and was surprised when he saw the archer was a young boy dressed in rags. The nobleman said "**You**! **You** did this? How did you develop such skill?" The lad replied "It's simple, your excellency. First, I take careful aim and then I let fly. After it hits the barn, I paint a target around it."

Jacob then told his friend that he worked the same way. Whenever he came across a good story, he remembered and used it for the appropriate occasion. Most of us don't have Jacob's memory, but we can write something down, store it in our word-processor or make a copy of an article and periodically go over it for use at the right time.

## FOUR CATEGORIES OF SPEECHES

We would like to describe four main types of speeches you may be required to give in class. They are: speeches to inform, speeches to persuade, speeches for special occasions, and group presentations. Each of these types has a different purpose. The kind of speech your professor assigns will be a controlling factor in how you develop the speech. Let's discuss each of these types of speeches.

### Speech to Inform

The speech to inform generally falls into two categories; a **demonstration speech** (or how to) or an **informative speech**. Although both speeches have as their general purpose to inform the audience, the demonstration speech actually requires you to show how something is done. Your task in a demonstration speech is to help your audience learn how to do something.

A demonstration speech usually requires props and other visual aids to demonstrate a technique. Demonstration speeches often fall flat when the presenter fails to adequately show how something is done and only describes a process verbally. For example, let's say you're going to demonstrate how to do western line dancing. If you only tell about line dancing, your audience could have a hard time understanding the steps of the dance. An effective demonstration gives the background on line dancing, demonstrates the basic line dance moves, plays the appropriate music to dance to, and perhaps allows members of the audience to get up and try the steps.

A straight **informative speech** does not require you to figuratively show or demonstrate something. In an informative speech you'll bring new and interesting information to an audience and help them to understand something better than they did before they heard your speech. Whether that be a specific conflict in the world, the risk of AIDS infection among college students, or the new book buy-back policy of the bookstore, the speaker needs to present information clearly, simply and establish the significance of the topic.

An informative speech often requires definitions and explanations. Definitions are needed to clarify any new or unusual terms and explanations are helpful in making the material more understandable. There are several methods that are helpful in giving explanations that your audience can both understand and retain. They are:

◆ Comparisons or analogies

◆ Examples or illustrations

◆ Statistics

Each allows your audience to view your topic as more concrete than an abstract explanation.

The following is an outline of an informative speech:

Purpose: To explain how to buy a camera that best fits someone's needs.

"YOUR BEST BET IN A CAMERA"

**INTRODUCTION**

I.   Attention Getting Device
     "Hold still and smile" (take a picture with a Polaroid)

II.  Orienting Material

   A.  I am an amateur photographer, and when I began I really didn't know what to buy.

   B.  Since then, I've learned that I could have saved a lot of time, money, and frustration with some information.

(Transition: What are your needs, concerns?  We'll look at two specific areas.)

**BODY**

Thesis Sentence: Let me describe for you how to select a camera that will fit your needs.

I.   First, what kinds of cameras are available to you today in the marketplace?

   A.  Looking at the automatic type camera.

   B.  There is also the instant development camera.

   C.  You may be interested in the 35 mm camera.

II.  Second, there are money considerations in terms of the pocketbook.

   A.  What features can someone expect for a $50 camera or less?

   B.  Look at the advantages and disadvantages of cameras over $100.

   C.  Other considerations to look at before buying.

     1.  Long range plans for the camera.

     2.  How expensive are accessories.

(Transition: These are some of the pieces of information you need to have before buying.)

## CONCLUSION

I.   SUMMARY

    A.  Remember that you have specific needs and have a number of cameras designed to meet those needs.

    B.  A salesman wants to sell you **his** needs.

    C.  With this information, now you can make a more informed and satisfied choice.

II.   CLOSING
Hold still, I want to remember you just as you are.
(Show the picture taken with Polaroid camera earlier.)

## The Persuasive Speech

Great persuaders throughout history have been able to use their rhetorical power to shape historic events. Pope Urban II did it in 1095 to launch the Crusades. Winston Churchill was able to rally the British people in 1940 to ward off the German threat against England. In 1960, John Kennedy was able to rouse the American people to a new standard of sacrifice in his famous inaugural address. Persuasive speeches take special skills. In this section, we look at some important principles to help you better prepare your own persuasive speech.

## Audience Analysis

If it's important to analyze your audience for the other kinds of speeches we've discussed so far—demonstration and informative—it's crucial to know your audience before you deliver a persuasive talk. If you advocate abolition of the death penalty and three quarters of your audience is strongly against your position, you stand little chance of turning them around in the short time you have to give the speech. If on the other hand, your audience slightly favors or is at least neutral toward your position, you have a better chance to persuade them.

Researchers in persuasion use a "semantic differential" to determine an audience's set of attitudes. Look at the scale below:

$$+3 \quad +2 \quad +1 \quad 0 \quad -1 \quad -2 \quad -3$$

Assume that zero represents a completely neutral attitude about some persuasive message. Let's say a typical college student has heard about the need to save and invest after graduation, but hasn't really worried about his financial future. Someone with a "plus 2" attitude would strongly believe that as soon as possible after graduation, she or he ought to start putting money away in an investment program. Someone with a "minus 2" attitude believes that investing is not that important when one is young. If the student speaker has determined that the audience ranges from plus 2 to minus 2, she has a good chance to change someone's attitude.

In his book *The Rhetoric*, Aristotle discusses the speaker, audience, and the speech. He provides a number of guidelines for preparing and delivering a persuasive speech but his most famous three are **ethos**, **pathos**, and **logos**. Ethos is the image of competence, integrity and rapport a speaker projects to an audience. Pathos refers to emotional appeal while logos includes logical arguments backed with supporting evidence. Let's look at each one so you can apply them as you prepare your own persuasion speech.

Think back on three of the most effective speakers you've ever heard either live or on television. What did they all have in common? They almost certainly came across as capable in their delivery and they really knew their subject. They were probably believable and they somehow bonded with their audience. Let's look at each of these facets of ethos.

## Competence

Competence is usually a combination of knowledge about the topic and a strong delivery. The speaker who has carefully researched the subject matter will usually come across as an expert. Let's take the student speaker who is advocating an investment program for college. If she has studied investment tactics, played the stock market, and had parents who invested wisely, she probably already knows quite a bit about her topic. If she does further research and pulls the research together in a well organized speech, she'll appear knowledgeable. If she adds to that a lively, polished and confident delivery, her chance of persuading increases even more. Many in an audience are more impressed by the speaker's delivery and seeming knowledge of a topic than they are by exactly what the speaker says.

## Pathos or Emotional Appeal

Most people buy products with emotion and later justify their purchase with logic. Have you ever bought something you really wanted with the lingering doubt that you really shouldn't have it but you want it so much you get it anyway? It could be a stereo, a car or some clothing. Your sense of reason might tell you that it's too expensive or you don't have the budget for it, but you desire it anyway. That's why most advertisers and salespeople appeal more to the **emotions** rather than reason—pathos often works better. Emotion can be used as a powerful tool in getting an audience to respond to a message. Typical emotions can be fear, joy, pity, or anger.

If you've seen the musical "The Music Man", you're aware of the scene where Professor Harold Hill gets the citizens of River City to worry about a pool table located in the middle of their town. He goes on to warn that many of the young boys are playing pool instead of doing their homework. He uses this pitch as a prelude for selling the townspeople on a boys' band—something he would like to lead and make money from. In his famous war speech, "Blood, Sweat and Tears", Winston Churchill was able to arouse the anger of the English people against the Germans. A logical approach might have worked but his riveting words galvanized the British into action.

One useful model for understanding emotional appeal is Abraham Maslow's famous pyramid included on p.16 of the interpersonal text.

At the bottom of the pyramid are physiological needs. The next step includes security needs. After that are affection needs, followed by esteem needs. The final one is self actualization. If a speaker has researched a topic carefully, he can tap into any one of those needs. Maslow maintained that the lower needs have to be satisfied before the upper ones. For example, if you're trying to address a hungry audience, you don't try to sell them on a program that will raise their self-esteem—but you could probably sell them hamburgers. If the lower needs are already met—physical, affection, self-esteem—but certain audience members feel something is missing in their lives, a speaker might appeal to their sense of self actualization. The slogan "Be All That You Can Be In the Army" is a typical example. Former Notre Dame football coach Lou Holtz is a master of spicing his speeches on self-actualization with emotional appeal. He can make an audience glide from humor to hope to anger back to humor as he promotes his messages about developing one's talent. As you prepare for your own speech, look for ways to involve the emotions of your audience.

## Logical Argument

Aristotle emphasized that one of the highest human faculties is the ability to reason. In his treatise on persuasion, *The Rhetoric*, Aristotle discusses the difference between the certain knowledge contained in pure logic and mathematics and the probable knowledge found in rhetoric. In math, you know that an answer to a problem is either correct or incorrect. If you've taken a critical thinking course, you also know that a categorical syllogism has parts that are either valid or invalid. A typical syllogism is:

All humans are mortal.

Beth is a human.

Therefore, she is mortal.

The major premise linked to the minor premise produces a certain conclusion. But in human activities, few things are absolutely certain. The best a persuader can do is to make a message appear highly **probable** to an audience. Reason gives us the chance to get as close as possible to certainty and truth even though we'll never achieve absolute certainty. For example, you can conclude that the syllogism about Beth is both valid and true: if she's human, she's also mortal. But juries and judges in a court case never know for certain whether people accused of crimes are really guilty even after a prosecutor has brought a case against them. Judges and juries will convict if prosecutors make it highly **probable** that a defendant is guilty as charged.

If your assignment is to present a speech supported by logical argument, you might use the same standard you would find in a court of law. You want to make your arguments as probable as possible. You do this by supporting your thesis with three kinds of evidence: factual, testimonial and statistical. Let's go back to the example of the student who is trying to convince her audience that it's wise to start investing money instead of buying on credit. She might have two basic arguments: (1) credit spending takes money **away** from a consumer (2) wise investment helps save and **produces** compound interest over time.

As stated above, both of these claims are only **assertions**. If she wants to **prove** her case, she can weave together facts, statistics and expert testimony about both of these contentions. For example, she can show how much people spend when they use credit cards and don't pay them off at the end of each month. She can go on to demonstrate with statistics that many people get so used to credit buying that they have no idea how much they're spending until they're deeply mired in debt. She can quote financial authorities who warn about the dangers of unwise credit spending.

In her second argument, she can show with an array of facts, statistics and expert testimony that money invested will yield solid returns over the years because of compound interest.

## Avoiding Defective Arguments

Speakers using logical argument should avoid **fallacies**. A fallacy is a form of defective thinking. For example, let's say a speaker claims that three out of five people in a group of 100 are happy with their living arrangements. To get this result, the interviewer talked to five people with three out of the five saying they were satisfied. The speaker would be guilty of a gross generalization based on an inadequate sample. If someone else attacked the credibility of an expert on a topic that had little to do with the person's expertise, she would be guilty of an "ad hominem" fallacy. She might say "This so-called expert can't be trusted when he talks about the national deficit because he smoked marijuana as a teenager." (You'll find a list of other fallacies on pp. 43-45 of the interpersonal text.)

As you prepare your own logical arguments, you might check to make sure you back your claims with sufficient evidence and that you avoid fallacies that could detract from your presentation.

## *Sample Outline for Persuasive Speech*

Following is an example of a speech outline utilizing logical argument. You might find it helpful as a model of blending pathos and logical argument.

Purpose: To convince listeners that finishing a college degree is well worth the effort both professionally and personally.

### INTRODUCTION

I.  The Path to Fulfillment

    A.  Imagine that for the next four years you could go on a journey:

        1.  battling windmills

        2.  hunting a white whale

        3.  meeting a Cyclops

        4.  along the way discover ideas that you never knew existed. (Change 8)

    B.  But wait—you are experiencing this journey right now in the form of a liberal arts education.

II. This road is at times long and hard. Many college students have asked themselves at one time or another one or both of these questions.

    A.  Why I am here?

    B.  Is this worth all the trouble?

### BODY

Thesis Sentence: Completing a college education yields rich rewards along the road of life both professionally and personally.

I.  A college degree yields many **professional** benefits.

    A.  You will make approximately 27-40% more money than a high school graduate

        1.  A man with four years of college can expect to earn between 1.19 million and 2.79 million dollars.

        2.  A male high school graduate can expect to make 860,000 to 1.87 million.

        3.  Lifetime earning for a woman with four years of college should be 520,000 to 1.2 million.

        4.  Female high school graduates earn from 380,000 to 800,000. (Higher Education and National Affairs 8)

    B.  A liberal arts degree will enable you to make valued contributions to the work force.

        1.  You will have a mastery of a variety of tasks.

        2.  Accustomed to a continuous learning environment

C. Have gained essential skills for the world of work

  1. Communication skills

    a. speaking

    b. listening

    c. editing

    d. critiquing

    e. interpreting

  2. Research skills

    a. collecting data

    b. analyzing

    c. synthesizing

    d. clarifying

    e. surveying

  3. Management skills

    a. planning

    b. organizing

    c. supervising

    d. developing

    e. delegating

    f. leading
(Salzman and Better 18)

D. Even when the economy is bad, graduates with liberal arts degrees fare well.

  1. During the depression, 92% of college graduates were employed.

  2. College graduates appear less frequently on, or are involved in:

    a. welfare rolls

    b. automobile accidents

    c. lower absentee rate than the rest of society
(Universal Higher Education Costs and Benefits 11)

II. The Liberal Arts will provide life-long **personal** benefits.

A. These studies help us when we are young and stay with us into our old age. They transcend our years on the college campus.

1. Literature

a. helps the mind to make more adequate judgments of beauty and ugliness.

b. helps distinguish between right and wrong

2. Arts

a. calls for the appreciation for the human experience through drama, novels, poetry, painting and sculpture.

b. strengthens and disciplines imagination which conditions moral insight.

3. Philosophy

a. understand human existence and experience in terms of value.

b. in terms of raw knowledge.

c. in context of beauty and creativity

d. understand reality as a whole

B. Knowledge is put into better order because of liberal education.

1. Ethics

a. sense of right and wrong

b. good and evil

c. allows the criteria by which one makes these decisions.

2. Natural Sciences

a. skills of accurate inquiry

b. experimental inquiry

**CONCLUSION**

I. Overall, the liberal arts curriculum will prepare the mind for the problems that one faces along the road of life.

A. You'll answer the question; is it worth it?

1. you'll make more money

2. master the skills that are increasingly valuable in a competitive job market.

3. analyze accurately and think clearly.

B. You'll answer the question; why am I here?

1. Many "white whales" are out there.

a. with knowledge you can overcome them and be a better person for it.

2. You will always keep on learning.

a. As Robert Frost said, "I took the road less traveled and that has made all the difference."

3. Keep learning for you never know where it might take you.

### Works Cited

"College Degrees Boost Lifetime Earnings, Census Bureau Reports." *Higher Education and National Affairs* April 22, 1983: 5.

"The Dangerous Myth of Over-education" *The Chronicle of Higher Education.* 11 November 1981: 56.

"Educational Authenticity." *Change Magazine* January-February 1986: 8-9.

Salzman, Marian and Nancy Better, *Wanted: Liberal Arts Graduates.* New York: Anchor Press, 1987.

St. Olaf College Self Study Committee. *Integration in the Christian Liberal Arts College.* Northfield, Minnesota: St. Olaf College Press, 1956.

"Universal Higher Education Costs and Benefits." Washington D.C., American Council on Higher Education, 1971.

## *Speeches for Special Occasions*

The speech of special occasion can take many forms. Among the most common are awards acceptance speeches, nomination speeches, eulogies, after-dinner speeches, graduation speeches, toasts, etc. These speeches are unique not only because of the setting of the speech, but also because of their purpose. Sometimes these speeches are testimonials to honor someone. Sometimes they are motivational and inspire the audience to do something. Sometimes they are humorous, allowing the audience to relax and enjoy a good funny story or comedic event. Sometimes speeches for special occasions have mixed purposes. A "Roast" is meant as an honor and testimonial but is intended to be humorous. Even a eulogy can have humorous moments. Let's look more closely at a speech of humor or **entertainment**.

Many public speakers try to be entertaining. Some succeed but many don't. A humorous speech is among the most difficult to give. Some try to tell risque stories and others try to string together a series of jokes. These often fall flat. A humorous speech relies on words, anecdotes, gestures, voice, unusual situations, pantomimes or a combination of these factors.

A humorous speech does not need to be a "belly buster." A speech to entertain might elicit smiles, chuckles, snickers, or grins of amusement. In fact, some call a speech to entertain a "speech to amuse." A humorous speech requires a speaker to catch the attention and interest of the audience and then hold their attention by developing a train of thought or an idea. One rule of thumb: don't tell a joke that hangs by itself. If it dies, you're left with no laughs. If your funny story or joke makes a point about the thesis of your speech, you can simply tie it to your theme and move on—whether you get laughs or not.

A speech to entertain is often given at dinners, club meetings, parties, and gatherings at which a weighty topic would be inappropriate and out of harmony with the occasion. In selecting a topic for a speech to entertain, the same criteria we have mentioned earlier in this chapter still apply.

### Group Presentations

Sometimes, students will deliver a group presentation to the rest of the class. This can take at least three forms: (1) a symposium, (2) a problem-solving format or (3) a meeting format. Let's look at each kind:

## Symposium

The goal of a symposium is to present information to an audience on a common topic. For example, five to seven people might examine close interpersonal relationships with particular emphasis on how they begin, how they develop and how they sometimes end. (Please refer to Chapter 9 of the Interpersonal text for more information on this subject.) After doing research on their own, members come together and pool their best ideas. This type of group can either present mini-speeches to the audience or can discuss a topic by interacting with each other in a discussion format.

## Problem Solving

A second kind of group presentation is the problem-solving exercise. Here, students get an assignment to research a problem and then go through the Reflective Thinking Agenda in an effort to work toward a solution. For example, the instructor may ask a group to try to solve a campus problem like parking for students or noise in the residence halls after 10 p.m. Or a teacher might ask groups to research and try to find solutions for national or international problems. Such problems could include gang violence among teens, date-rape on college campuses or the threat of small countries getting nuclear weapons.

The steps of John Dewey's Reflective Thinking Agenda are listed below:

1. Describe the symptoms of the problem

2. Find out what's causing it

3. Establish criteria for solving it

4. Brainstorm for solutions that best fit the criteria

5. Find solutions that best fit the criteria

To illustrate how this process works, let's say the problem is one of too few parking places on campus to accommodate students, staff, faculty and administrators. In step one, members present information on the symptoms of the problem. These could include students complaining about the lack of places to park, faculty grumbling about someone parking in their parking lot or the number of tickets given by campus security. In the next step, the group tries to pin-point why the problem is occurring. Such causes could be too little space near classroom buildings or a perception by many that they deserve to park within a block of their classes based on the tuition they're paying.

Then the group moves on to a discussion of **criteria.** Criteria are those standards that help insure that a problem gets solved. For example, if you were buying a used car and you were limited to $4,000, your criteria might be good gas mileage and dependable service. For the parking problem, the criteria could be that whatever solution is recommended, both faculty and students should be accommodated within two blocks of their classrooms or offices and the plan should not cost more than $10,000 to implement.

In the next stage, members **brainstorm** solutions. In brainstorming, participants suggest possible solutions without analyzing each one in detail. In the final phase, members critically look at each proposal and decide whether it fits the criteria they all agreed on. For example, if two people recommend a new parking garage, there is no way one can be built for $10,000. Or if someone else urges that faculty be given first priority, that solution would not fit the first criterion.

## Meeting Format

A final kind of discussion could be a meeting format. Here members go through an agenda of subjects and make decisions. For example, the student government wants to plan on the number and types of invited speakers for the following academic year. Their agenda could include:

1. What will the current budget allow?

2. What kind of qualifications would students want in speakers?

3. Who will get the information about speaker availability?

4. How will the events be advertised to the student body?

5. How will we get feedback on each speech?

Often, an organization will utilize Roberts' Rules of Order to make sure agenda items are handled efficiently and everyone has a chance to speak.

In all three styles, members should try to deal with material efficiently and use intelligent reasoning to come to decisions. They should also avoid **groupthink**—the tendency to go along with the flow of what everyone else is thinking no matter how illogical it might be.

## SUMMARY

In this section we have described various approaches to public speaking and explained four different categories of speeches. All four types have some elements in common. Each should be well organized, carefully researched and skillfully presented. In the next section we'll offer some criteria for evaluating speeches.

# SECTION VI

## *Criteria for Evaluating Speeches*

**Preview**  In this section, you will:

◆ Understand the importance of speech criticism in developing your speaking skills.

◆ See the relationship between speech criticism and your critical reasoning ability.

◆ Be able to use the guidelines given for content, organization, and delivery in critiquing your own and others public speaking efforts.

*Speak the speech, I pray you, as I pronounced it to you, trippingly on the tongue; but if you mouth it, as many of your players do, I has as lief the town-crier spoke my lines. Nor do not saw the air too much with your hand, thus; but use all gently: for in the very torrent, tempest, and - as I may say - whirlwind of passion, you must acquire and beget a temperance, that may give it smoothness.*

*- Shakespeare*

It is important that you develop adequate skills for speech criticism.  Being able to critique a speech helps you plan and organize your own speeches more effectively and at the same time contributes to each class member's growth.  Also, as you develop your speech criticism skills, you are developing the critical reasoning skills we discussed in Chapter Two of the interpersonal textbook.

## SPEECH EVALUATION

The three most important areas of speech evaluation include content, organization, and delivery.  In the appendix we have included several different examples of speech criticism forms.  However, we believe the following questions are solid guidelines you should ask yourself as you practice your speech.  These are also the general criteria you would utilize for evaluating other speeches.

## Content

- ◆ Was the topic appropriate for the audience: did it have depth and/or was it innovative?
- ◆ Did the speaker analyze and adapt to the audience?
- ◆ Was the topic specific enough/limited in scope?
- ◆ Were the main points fully developed?
- ◆ Did the speaker establish her own credibility?
- ◆ Were logical and/or emotional appeals effective?
- ◆ Was vivid, descriptive language used?
- ◆ Did the speaker use visual aids to help clarify points?
- ◆ Were the audience questions effectively answered?
- ◆ Did the speech conform to the assignment?

## Organization

- ◆ Did the introduction clarify the topic and capture interest?
- ◆ Did the speaker use any devices for illustration and development?
- ◆ Were the transitions effective?
- ◆ Was the speech clearly organized?
- ◆ Did the conclusion summarize the main points and leave the audience with a final, specific thought?

## Delivery

- ◆ Did the speaker dress appropriately for the occasion?
- ◆ Was the speaker's posture straight and non-distracting?
- ◆ Did the speaker relax and use natural body movements?
- ◆ Did the speaker maintain good visual interaction with his or her audience?
- ◆ Did the speaker use expressive and appropriate gestures?
- ◆ Was the speaker fluid and articulate?

◆ Did the speaker use adequate volume and vocal variety?

◆ Was the speaker in overall control of the topic and convey a desire to communicate?

## Summary

Being able to evaluate your speeches and others is part of the process of becoming an effective speaker. The list above should help you in the process, but don't be limited by it. Add other criteria that you, your professor and the members of your class believe are helpful. The most important step is for you to critically evaluate your speech before you deliver it. Don't be overly hard on yourself, but don't let yourself off the hook. Do the best you can with the material you have. Don't allow speech criticism to be personal. The purpose of speech criticism in a speech course should always be aimed at helping the speaker improve his or her speaking ability. Your speech course is a laboratory to experiment and polish your speaking skills. Make the most of it and enjoy.

# APPENDICES

# APPENDIX A

## TOPIC SUGGESTIONS

## INFORMATION SPEECHES

### Demonstration/Processes

C.P.R.

Researching Genealogy

How to roof and put siding on a house

Card tricks

Clogging

Tap dancing

How to deliver a baby

How to change a tire

How to inject insulin

Knitting

Crocheting

Cleaning and polishing shoes

Oil changing

Ironing

How to cook well and easily with a microwave

Bingo

Technical theater lighting

Commercial fishing knots

Taking pictures

How to tie an ascot tie

How to make your favorite dish

Choosing a diamond

Origami

Tie dyeing

Getting around in college bookstores

How to be an informed spectator at a concert (classical, rock, etc.)

How to fire a missile

How to catch trains in a foreign country

Window painting

How to be a good employee

How to look for a job

### World Events: General Information

Tianamen Square Massacre

Vietnam War

Watergate

Iran-Contra scandal

Gulf War

Holocaust

Whitewater scandal

Kennedy assassination

Lincoln assassination

## Science and Medicine

Photosynthesis

Paternity testing

Artificial insemination

Cloning

Grafting

Transplanting organs

CAT scan

Finding organ donors

DNA/RNA replication

How a virus/bacteria work to get you sick

Recombinant DNA

## Government/Politics

How a bill becomes law

Presidential succession

Impeachment of a president

Trial for espionage/treason

Confirmation process of a presidential appointee

Socialist Government

Communist Government

Monarchy

Oligarchy

Anarchy

Dictatorship

How to register to vote

Checks and balances system

Electoral College

College of Cardinals/How they select a Pope

How to determine constitutionality

## Sports

Crew racing

Soccer

Tennis

Free throw shooting

Horseback riding

Pickleball

Racquetball

Fencing

Karate

Exercising

Dancing

Hunting

Golf

Jogging

Rugby

Lacrosse

Hang Gliding

## Miscellaneous

How to buy and put in contact lenses

Finding your way in a subway system

Getting a passport

Armed Forces security check

## News and Information

Fax transmission

Operating the Internet

How the Associated Press wire works

Satellite transmission operation

Circulation of a newspaper

Pirate radio stations

Guidelines to getting on the air

How your TV produces an image

TV News: It's more than it looks

# PERSUASIVE SPEECH TOPICS

## Controversies

Alcohol and drug use

AIDS testing

Abortion vs. Right to Life

Adoption vs. surrogacy

Advertising

American education system

Birth control in high schools

Black market babies

Cocaine and crack

Creationism vs. Evolutionism

Capital punishment

Collegiate athletics

Discrimination

Drinking and driving

Drugs and sports

Divorce

Euthanasia

Education financing

Fundamentalism vs. Humanism

Free speech and responsibility

Gay Rights

Grading systems

Gun control

Homosexuality

Prejudice

Pornography

Prostitution

Population controls

Public vs. private education

Teenage parenting

Television violence

Religion in public schools

Women as Catholic priests

## Medical Issues

Giving blood: why do it?

Donating organs

C.P.R. certification

Preventing heart disease

Dental care

Dangers of smoking/chewing tobacco

Drink more water

Steroid use

Caffeine consumption

Sodium intake

Sugar blues

Dieting for health

Cloning

Smoking

Vegetarianism vs. meat consumption

Cholesterol intake

Fat intake

Benefits of chemical free fruits and vegetables

Regular exercise

Importance of health insurance

Health Care Reform

## Political Issues

Offshore oil drilling on the West Coast

Improved athletic programs

Improving Higher Education

School financing

Affirmative Action

Apartheid

Liberalism vs. Conservatism

Dairy price supports

Drinking age

Espionage

55 mph speed limit

Nuclear arms in the hands of Third World countries

Strategic Defense Initiative

Trade tariffs

Unions vs. Management

Voting responsibility

Israel: Arabs and Jews in conflict

Violence and the Olympics

Prominent political figures and controversy

Presidential scandals

Peace-time draft

Human rights violations

Palestinian Liberation Movement

Economic control and inflation

Right to privacy

North American Free Trade Agreement

Favored Nation Status

## Issues from Hobbies

Tanning bed safety

Magic tricks—the hand is quicker than the eye

Vegetarians vs. carnivores

Sports relieve stress

Techo Music

Classical music

Interactive computing

Sign language

Tennis

Badmitten

Skiing

Surfing

Skiing

Hiking

Rock climbing

## *Miscellaneous*

Drinking and driving

Liability of bars and taverns

Wearing seatbelts

Racial desegregation

TV news

Children's advertising

Forestry issues

Child abuse

Time management

Day care centers

Money management

Liberal Art Education

Cohabitation

Faculty tenure: should we allow it?

Semester vs. quarter system

Importance of speaking a foreign language

Why not to play a certain sport

Why not to have a roommate

Why living in a house is better than living in residence halls

Why everyone should read _____ (book title)

## SPECIAL OCCASION SPEECHES

Toasts

Roasts

Tributes

Eulogies

Introduction

Personal opinion

Current event

Nostalgic (recounting an event in the past)

Vision of the Future

Humorous speech

Acceptance

After-dinner

Graduation

Anniversary

Wedding

Retirement

# APPENDIX B

## PREPARING THE SPEECH

I. Preparation process

    A. Analyze your particular audience: what would they find interesting and useful?

    B. Pick a topic.

    C. Narrow it according to the time you have.

    D. Write a one page outline based on what you know already about the topic.

    E. Research materials.

    F. Compose a two to four page outline depending on the length of project.

        1. Begin with your central idea sentence.

        2. Write introduction and conclusion *after* the body of the presentation.

        3. Make sure the introduction is a "grabber."

    G. Review and polish into a final draft.

II. Techniques of memory

    A. "Energizer effect"—or why it helps to be nervous

    B. Components of memory

        1. association (linking images)

        2. imagination (seeing vivid images)

        3. repetition: the importance of rehearsal for oral presentations

III. Practical tips

    A. Speak to communicate clearly rather than to impress.

        1. Speak in direct sentences.

        2. Provide concrete examples to illustrate principles.

    B. Vocal aspects:

        1. Speak more slowly than usual to take advantage of the differential between thought speed and voice speed.

        2. Project your voice.

# APPENDIX C

## POSSIBLE LIBRARY RESOURCES

**A Matter of Fact: A Digest of Current Facts, With Citations to Sources**
This source contains full-text abstracts of statistical statements related to current social, economic, political, health, and environmental public policy issues.

**Opposing Viewpoints series**
This series presents both sides of issues, each volume covering a separate issue.

**Reader's Guide to Periodical Literature**
This source indexes scholarly and general interest periodicals and covers many subject areas.

**Expanded Academic Index (1984 - present)**
This database indexes scholarly and general interest journals in the social sciences, humanities, and general sciences.

**Uncover**
This database contains tables of contents of more than 10,000 recent journals. Document delivery of articles located in Uncover is available for a fee.

**Facts on File**
This database summarizes all key U.S. and international news developments as reported in major newspapers and news magazines. The database contains the full text of all Facts on File issues from January 1990 to the present. The information is updated each week.

**National Newspaper Index**
This index covers all current news reported in 5 major U.S. newspapers.

**Current Newspapers**

    The Wall Street Journal

    The New York Times

    The Christian Science Monitor

    The Washington Post

    The Los Angeles Times

# Appendix D

## Format for Sample Speech Outline

Title:

Purpose Statement:

I.  Introduction

    A.  Attention Getter

    B.  Relate to Yourself (credibility)

    C.  Relate to Audience (why should they listen or care)

    D.  Preview Main Points (what you will discuss in the speech)

**Thesis Sentence**

II.  Body

    A.  First Main Point

        1.  Supporting Material

        2.  Supporting Material

    B.  Second Main Point

        1.  Supporting Material

        2.  Supporting Material

    C.  Third Main Point

        1.  Supporting Material

        2.  Supporting Material

III.  Conclusion

    A.  Signal End

    B.  Review Main Points

    C.  Clincher

IV.  List of Works Cited

# APPENDIX E

## Speech Evaluation Form

Speaker _____

Evaluator _____

Grade _____

| Superior | Very Good | Good | Needs Much Work | Organization | Comments |
|---|---|---|---|---|---|
| | | | | **Introduction** | |
| | | | | Gets attention | |
| | | | | Rapport with audience | |
| | | | | States purpose/central idea | |
| | | | | Transitions to Body | |
| | | | | **Body** | |
| | | | | Main points clear/organized | |
| | | | | Outline format | |
| | | | | Content | |
| | | | | Development of key points | |
| | | | | **Conclusion** | |
| | | | | Summary/Review | |
| | | | | Compelling Final Statement | |
| | | | | **Delivery** | |
| | | | | **Verbal** | |
| | | | | Projection | |
| | | | | Voice rate | |
| | | | | Voice pitch/variety | |
| | | | | Articulation | |
| | | | | Quality | |
| | | | | **Nonverbal** | |
| | | | | Appearance: outfit appropriate to the occasion | |
| | | | | Eye contact | |
| | | | | Gestures | |
| | | | | Body language | |
| | | | | Smile/Facial expression | |
| | | | | **Visual Aids** | |
| | | | | Blended with speech | |
| | | | | Handling during talk | |

**Summary Comments:**

# APPENDIX F

## TWO GROUP DISCUSSION MODELS

## PROBLEM SOLVING

I.  Steps:

   A.  Sign up for a topic in class

   B.  Do research on your topic

      1.  Refer to the sheet describing sources in Foley (included in Appendix)

      2.  Feel free to share sources with other members of your group

   C.  Meet outside of class with your group to plan a lively, educational and entertaining discussion

   D.  Have a 30 minute discussion in class

I.  Requirements:

   A.  A two-page outline to be presented to the instructor at the beginning of your discussion

      1.  Should have an introduction, a body and a conclusion

      2.  Should reflect the research you did on your topic

   B.  Active participation in the group session

I.  Grading criteria:

   A.  Solid participation in the discussion with an obvious knowledge of the following:

      1.  The Reflective Thinking Agenda (RTA)

      2.  The ability to state your ideas clearly

      3.  Familiarity with the topic based on your research

      4.  Idea clash when appropriate

      5.  Listening skills

   B.  A carefully prepared, typed outline with a list of sources on the last page

# GROUP PROCESS PRESENTATION

1.  Choose a topic dealing with communication (start with your course textbook). Narrow the topic to an acceptable size.

2.  Do research on the topic.

3.  Identify a presentation mode that is creative, unusual, unique and interesting. Let your imagination be your guide.

4.  Modify your topic to the presentation or modify your presentation to the topic.

5.  Compile a **group** outline. **Type** it and make sure it is in complete sentence form. The outline is due just prior to your presentation. Also include an analysis of your group's behavior and process. This must be written individually by every group member as an addition to the outline. This individual report will be graded, thus producing an individual grade as well as a group grade. The report should be two pages in length, essay style and in typed form. It should analyze the group: composition, problem solving behaviors, decision-making abilities, communication techniques and effectiveness. The report should highlight any positive and/or negative aspects of the group's behavior.

6.  Rehearse the presentation.

7.  **Every** group member must take an active part in the presentation.

8.  Present the group project to the class. Presentation time is 15 minutes total.

# APPENDIX G

**Persuasive Speech Evaluation Form**

Speaker _____

Evaluator _____

Grade _____

What did you especially like? _____

_____

In your opinion, how could the speech be improved? _____

_____

| Superior | Very Good | Good | Needs Much Work | PLEASE COMMENT ON ANY OF THE FOLLOWING AREAS (BE SPECIFIC) | COMMENTS |
|---|---|---|---|---|---|
| | | | | Did the speaker formulate an effective persuasive strategy? | |
| | | | | Did the speaker establish ethos? | |
| | | | | Did the speaker analyze and adapt to audience? | |
| | | | | Were arguments supported with enough evidence? | |
| | | | | Were emotional appeals effective? | |
| | | | | Did the speaker appear to have a clear persuasive purpose? | |
| | | | | Did the speaker establish "common ground" with the audience? | |

**Summary Comments:**

# Appendix H

## Bibliographical Formats

The two most widely used bibliographic formats in universities are the **MLA** format (Modern Language Association) and the **APA** format (American Psychological Association). For explicit details see the MLA or APA guides. A sample of each format follows.

**MLA format**: For most books, arrange the information into three parts, each followed by a period: (1) the author's name, last first; (2) the title and subtitle, underlined; and, (3) the place of publication, the publisher, and the date. Arrange the list in alphabetical order by author.

### ONE AUTHOR
Powell, John, S.J. <u>Why Am I Afraid To Tell You Who I Am?</u> Chicago: Argus Communications, 1969.

### TWO OR MORE AUTHORS
Caputo, John, Hazel, Harry, and Colleen McMahon. <u>Interpersonal Communication: Competency Through Critical Thinking</u>. Needham Heights, MA.: Allyn and Bacon Publishing, 1994.

### UNKNOWN AUTHOR
<u>The Times Atlas of the World</u>. 8th ed. New York: New York Times, 1990.

### PERIODICAL
Burgoon, Judee K., and Joseph B. Walther. "Nonverbal Expectations and the Evaluative Consequence of Violations." <u>Human Communication Research</u>, 17-2 (1990), 232-265.

### "MLA Format" Bibliography

Burgoon, Judee K., and Joseph B. Walther. "Nonverbal Expectations and the Evaluative Consequence of Violations." <u>Human Communication Research</u>, 17-2 (1990), 232-265.

Caputo, John, Hazel, Harry, and Colleen McMahon. <u>Interpersonal Communication: Competency Through Critical Thinking</u>. Needham Heights, MA.: Allyn and Bacon Publishing, 1994.

Powell, John, S.J. <u>Why Am I Afraid To Tell You Who I Am?</u> Chicago: Argus Communications, 1969.

<u>The Times Atlas of the World</u>. 8th ed. New York: New York Times, 1990.

**APA Format**. The alphabetical list of works cited is entitled "References." References are listed in alphabetical order with: (1) the last name of the author first, (2) date of publication in parentheses and a period; (3) The title is written with only the first word capitalized and the entire title italicized; and (4) the place of publication and the publisher.

**ONE AUTHOR**
Powell, J. (1969). *Why am I afraid to tell you who I am?* Chicago: Argus Communications.

**TWO OR MORE AUTHORS**
Caputo, J., Hazel, H. & McMahon, C. (1994). *Interpersonal communication: Competency through critical thinking.* Needham Heights: Allyn & Bacon Publishing.

**UNKNOWN AUTHOR**
*The Times atlas of the world* (1990). 8th ed. New York: New York Times.

**PERIODICAL**
Burgoon, J.K. & Walther, J.B. (1990). Nonverbal expectations and the evaluative consequence of violations. *Human Communication Research,* 17 (2), 232-265.

### "APA Format" References

Burgoon, J.K. & Walther, J.B. (1990). Nonverbal expectations and the evaluative consequence of violations. *Human Communication Research,* 17 (2), 232-265.

Caputo, J., Hazel, H. & McMahon, C. (1994). *Interpersonal communication: Competency through critical thinking.* Needham Heights: Allyn & Bacon Publishing.

Powell, J. (1969). *Why am I afraid to tell you who I am?* Chicago: Argus Communications.

*The Times atlas of the world* (1990). 8th ed. New York: New York Times.